The GROSSEST JOKES EVER!

h
hinkler

yuck!

Ick!

Eww!

hinkler

Published by Hinkler Pty Ltd
45–55 Fairchild Street
Heatherton Victoria 3202 Australia
www.hinkler.com

© Hinkler Pty Ltd 2004, 2010, 2014, 2021, 2022

Cover design: Hinkler Studio
Illustrations: Glen Singleton
Joke collection: Nicolas Brasch, Barb Whiter and Katie Hewat

ISBN: 978 1 4889 4668 4

Printed and bound in China

CONTENTS

Riddles, Riddles, Riddles

1   **W**hat's green, sticky and smells like eucalyptus?
Koala vomit.

2   **W**hat do termites eat for dessert?
Toothpicks.

3   **W**hy did Piglet look in the toilet?
He was looking for Pooh.

4   **W**hat do you call a long, thin booger?

Slim Pickins.

5   **W**hat's a pig's snot called?

Ham boogers.

6   **M**ummy, Mummy, can I lick the bowl?

No! You'll have to flush like everyone else.

7   **W**hat's the difference between beans and boogers?

Kids never want to eat their beans.

8   **W**hy do elephants have trunks?

Because they can't fit everything into a handbag.

9   **W**hat did the toothpick say to the booger?
What are you doing here?

10   **W**hy do ninja's farts smell so bad?
They're silent but deadly.

11   **W**hat's made of leather and smells like a sneeze?
A shoe.

12   **H**ow does a monster count to thirteen?
On his fingers.

13   **W**hy shouldn't you fart in an elevator?
It's just wrong on so many levels.

14   **D**id you hear about the secret agent who farted in her sleep?
She blew her cover.

15   **W**hat did the woman at the diarrhoea call centre say?
Can you hold, please?

16   **W**hy did your sister put her socks on inside out?

Because there was a hole on the outside.

17   **W**hy did the driver fart in his wallet?

He needed gas money.

18   **W**hat happens if it stings when you wee?

Urine trouble.

19   **W**hat happens when you're late to a cannibal party?

They give you the cold shoulder.

20   **W**hy are fart jokes better than eye jokes?

Eye jokes are cornea.

21 **W**hat's the difference between school lunches and a pile of slugs?

School lunches are on plates.

22 **W**hat did the boy say after eating a booger?

You might think it's funny, but it's snot.

23 **W**hat did the royal taster say after drinking the poisoned water?

Not much!

24 **W**hat did Spartacus say to the cannibal who ate his wife?

Nothing. He was gladiator.

25 **W**hich area of the police force accepts monkeys?

The Special Branch.

26 **A**re fart jokes acceptable?

As long as they don't stink.

27 **W**hat did the first mate see in the toilet?

The captain's log.

28 **W**hy do hot dogs have such bad manners?
They spit in the frying pan.

29 **W**hich kind of poo smells better than it tastes?
Shampoo.

30 **W**hat did the booger say to the finger?
Pick on someone your own size.

31   **W**hy wasn't the butterfly invited to the dance?

Because it was a moth ball.

32   **W**ho doesn't like fart jokes?

People with no scents of humour.

Poking Fun at Teachers

33 **S**cience teacher: *'What are nitrates?'*

Student: *'Cheaper than day rates.'*

34 **E**nglish teacher: *'Jamie, give me a sentence beginning with "I".'*

Jamie: *'I is …'.*

Teacher: *'No Jamie, you must always say "I am".'*

Jamie: *'Okay. I am the ninth letter of the alphabet.'*

35 **H**istory teacher: *'What's a Grecian urn?'*

Student: *'About $500 a week.'*

36 **W**hat's the difference between a train station and a teacher?

One minds the train, the other trains the mind.

37 **D**id you hear about the maths teacher who wanted to order pizza for dinner, but was divided about whether to have additional cheese?

38 **T**eacher: *'Did you know the bell had gone?'*
Sue: *'I didn't take it, Miss.'*

39 **H**istory teacher: *'What was Camelot?'*
Student: *'A place where camels are parked.'*

40 **T**eacher: *'If I bought 100 buns for a dollar, what would each bun be?'*
Student: *'Stale.'*

41 **T**eacher: *'Wally, why are you late?'*
Wally: *'The train had a flat tyre.'*

42 **H**istory teacher: *'What's the best thing about history?'*
Mary: *'All the dates.'*

43 In which class do you learn how to shop for bargains?

Buy-ology.

44 '**M**ary,' said her teacher. *'You can't bring that lamb into class. What about the smell?'*

'Oh, that's all right Miss,' replied Mary. 'It'll soon get used to it.'

45 '**W**hat are three words most often used by students?' the teacher asked the class.

'I don't know,' sighed a student.

'That's correct!' said the teacher.

46 **S**hane: *'Dad, today my teacher yelled at me for something I didn't do.'*

Dad: 'What did he yell at you for?'

Shane: 'For not doing my homework.'

47 **W**hen George left school he was going to be a printer.

All his teachers said he was the right type.

48 **T**eacher: *'What came after the Stone Age and the Bronze Age?'*

Student: 'The saus-age.'

49 Principal: *'You should have been here at 9.00.'*
Student: *'Why, what happened?'*

50 Mother: *'Did you get a good place in the geography test?'*
Daughter: *'Yes, I sat next to the cleverest kid in the class.'*

Are you sure that's the right answer? Just remember.. if you get it wrong... .. SO DO I !

51 Teacher: *'That's three times I've asked you a question. Why won't you reply?'*
Student: *'Because you told me not to answer you back.'*

52 Geography teacher: *'What's the coldest country in the world?'*
Student: *'Chile.'*

53 How many aerobic teachers does it take to change a light bulb?

Five, one to change it, the others to say, 'A Little to the left, a little to the right, a little to the left, a little to the right.'

You look so cold...you must surely be from Chile...or Alaska ...or Siberia.

No ...I pack the frozen peas down at the local supermarket!

54 **H**istory teacher: *'Here is a question to check that you did your homework on British kings and queens. Who came after Mary?'*

Student: *'Her little lamb.'*

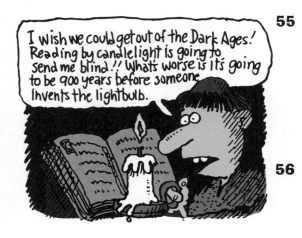

55 **H**istory teacher: *'Why do we refer to the period around 1000 years AD as the Dark Ages?'*

Student: *'Because there were so many knights.'*

56 **W**hen Dad came home, he was amazed to see his son sitting on a horse, writing something. *'What are you doing up there?'* he asked.

'Well, the teacher told us to write an essay on our favourite animal,' replied the boy.

57 **W**hy did the teacher wear sunglasses?

Because his students were so bright.

58 **C**ookery teacher: *'Helen, what are the best things to put in a fruit cake?'*

Helen: *'Teeth!'*

59 **D**id you hear about the cross-eyed teacher?
He couldn't control his pupils.

60 **F**ather: *'I want to take my girl out of this terrible maths class.'*
Teacher: *'But she's top of the class!'*
Father: *'That's why it must be a terrible class!'*

61 **T**eacher: *'I'd like you to be very quiet today, girls. I've got a dreadful headache.'*
Mary: *'Please Miss, why don't you do what Mum does when she has a headache?'*
Teacher: *'What's that?'*
Mary: *'She sends us out to play!'*

62 **M**aths teacher: *'Paul. If you had five pieces of chocolate and Sam asked for one of them, how many would you have left?'*
Paul: *'Five.'*

Would you fancy a piece of my chocolate?

URRRR... NO THANKS

63 **T**eacher: *'I hope I didn't see you copying from John's exam paper, James.'*
James: *'I hope you didn't see me either!'*

64 **W**hat is the robot teacher's favourite part of the day?

Assembly.

65 **W**hat is the easiest way to get a day off school?

Wait until Saturday.

66 **S**cience teacher: *'Which travels faster, heat or cold?'*

Student: *'Heat, because you can catch a cold.'*

67 **W**hat would you get if you crossed a teacher with a vampire?

Lots of blood tests.

68 **S**tudent to teacher: *'I don't want to worry you but my dad said that if my grades don't improve, someone's going to get a spanking.'*

69 **T**eacher: *'What's the name of a liquid that won't freeze?'*
Student: *'Hot water.'*

70 **T**eacher: *'Can anyone tell me what the Dog Star is?'*
Student: *'Lassie.'*

71 Teacher: *'I wish you'd pay a little attention.'*

Student: *'I'm paying as little attention as possible.'*

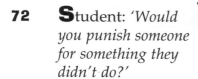

72 Student: *'Would you punish someone for something they didn't do?'*

Teacher: *'Of course not.'*

Student: *'Good, because I didn't do my homework.'*

73 Teacher: *'Billy, stop making ugly faces at the other students!'*

Billy: *'Why?'*

Teacher: *'Well, when I was your age, I was told that if I kept making ugly faces, my face would stay that way.'*

Billy: *'Well, I can see you didn't listen.'*

74 **H**ave you heard about the gym teacher who ran around exam rooms, hoping to jog students' memories?

75 ... **O**r, the craft teacher who had her pupils in stitches?

76 ... **O**r, maybe, the cookery teacher who thought Hamlet was an omelette with bacon?

77 **D**ad: *'How did you find your maths exam?'*
Son: *'Unfortunately, it wasn't lost!'*

78 **W**hat is an English teacher's favourite fruit?
The Grapes of Wrath.

79 **T**eacher: *'Why can't you answer any of my questions in class?'*
Student: *'If I could, there wouldn't be much point in me being here.'*

80 **T**eacher: *'What family does the octopus belong to?'*
Student: *'Nobody's I know.'*

81 **W**hy can you believe everything a bearded teacher tells you?
They can't tell bare-faced lies.

82 **D**id you hear about the two history teachers who were dating?

They go to restaurants to talk about old times.

83 **W**hy are maths teachers good at solving detective stories?

Because they know when all the clues add up.

84 **W**hat do you call a teacher with a school on his head?

Ed.

85 **T**eacher to parent: *'David's career choice as a train driver will suit him well. He has more experience of lines than any other student at this school!'*

86 First teacher: *'What's wrong with young Jimmy today? I saw him running around the playground, screaming and pulling at his hair.'*

Second teacher: *'Don't worry. He's just lost his marbles.'*

87 What word is always spelled wrong?

Wrong.

88 Maths teacher: *'Anne, why have you brought a picture of the queen of England with you today?'*

Anne: *'You told us to bring a ruler with us.'*

89 Maths teacher: *'Richard, if you had 50 cents in each trouser pocket, and $2 in each blazer pocket, what would you have?'*

Richard: *'Someone else's uniform, Sir.'*

90 What kind of tests do witch teachers give?

Hex-aminations.

91 Student: *'I don't think I deserve a zero on this test.'*

Teacher: *'No, neither do I but it was the lowest I could give you!'*

92 **W**hy didn't the fart go to school?

Because it got expelled.

93 **M**aths teacher: *'If you multiplied 1386 by 395, what would you get?'*

Student: *'The wrong answer.'*

94 **T**eacher: *'Billy, did you pick your nose?''*

Billy: *'No, I was born with it.'*

95 **'O**ur teacher talks to herself in class, does yours?'

'Yes, but she doesn't realise it. She thinks we're listening!'

96 **P**laying truant from school is like having a credit card.

Lots of fun now, pay later.

97 **L**augh, and the class laughs with you.

But you get detention alone.

98 **S**tudent: *'I didn't do my homework because I lost my memory.'*

Teacher: *'When did this start?'*

Student: *'When did what start?'*

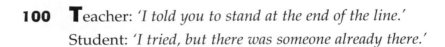

99 **W**hat do you call a teacher who won't fart in public?

A private tutor.

100 **T**eacher: *'I told you to stand at the end of the line.'*

Student: *'I tried, but there was someone already there.'*

101 **T**eacher: *'Why didn't you answer me, Stuart?'*

Stuart: *'I did, I shook my head.'*

Teacher: *'You don't expect me to hear it rattling from here, do you?'*

102 **T**eacher: *'I said to draw a cow eating grass, but you've only drawn a cow.'*

Student: *'Yes, the cow has eaten all the grass.'*

103 **T**eacher: *'How dare you fart in front of me!'*

Student: *'Sorry, Sir. I didn't realise it was your turn next.'*

104 **T**eacher: *'Why haven't you been to school for the last two weeks, Billy?'*

Billy: *'It's not my fault – whenever I go to cross the road outside, there's a man with a sign saying '"Stop Children Crossing"!'*

105 **D**id you hear about the teacher who wore sunglasses to give out exam results?

He took a dim view of his students' performance.

106 **H**istory teacher: *'Why were ancient sailing ships so eco-friendly?'*

Student: *'Because they could go for hundreds of miles to the galleon.'*

107 Teacher: *'What's the name of a bird that doesn't build its own nest?'*

Student: *'The cuckoo.'*

Teacher: *'That's right – how did you know that?'*

Student: *'Easy, Sir, everyone knows cuckoos live in clocks!'*

108 How does a maths teacher know how long she sleeps?

She takes a ruler to bed.

109 Did you hear about the technology teacher who left teaching to try to make something of himself?

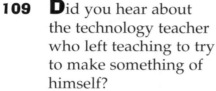

110 Why did the boy throw his watch out of the window during an exam?

Because he wanted to make time fly.

111 English teacher: *'James, give me a sentence with the word "counterfeit" in it.'*

James: *'I wasn't sure if she was a centipede or a millipede, so I had to count her feet.'*

112 What did the booger say to the school desk?

I'm stuck on you!

113 '**W**hat were you before you came to school, girls and boys?' asked the teacher, hoping that someone would say 'babies'. She was disappointed when all the children cried out, 'Happy!'

114 **S**tudent 1: 'We bought our retiring science teacher a gift – toilet water that cost $20.'

Student 2: 'What! I would've sold you water from our toilets for only $2!'

115 **T**eacher: 'That's the stupidest boy in the whole school.'

Mother: 'That's my son.'

Teacher: 'Oh! I'm so sorry.'

Mother: 'You're sorry!'

116 '**I** hope you're not one of those boys who sits and watches the school clock,' said the principal to the new boy.

'No, Sir,' he replied. 'I've got a digital watch that beeps at three-fifteen!'

117 **T**eacher: 'Your daughter's only five and she can spell her name backwards! Why, that's remarkable!'

Mother: 'Yes, we're very proud of her.'

Teacher: 'And what is your daughter's name?'

Mother: 'Anna.'

118 '**H**ow old would you say I am, Francis?' the teacher asked.

'Forty,' said the boy promptly.

'What makes you think I'm forty?' asked the puzzled teacher.

'My big brother is twenty,' he replied, 'and you're twice as silly as he is!'

119 **M**y teacher says I've got such bad handwriting that I ought to be a doctor!

120 '**D**o you like your new school, Billy?' asked Uncle Ned.

'Sometimes,' said the boy.

'When is that?'

'When it's closed!'

121 **B**en's teacher thinks Ben is a wonder child.

She wonders whether he'll ever learn anything.

122 '**I**'m not going to school today,' said Alexander to his mother. 'The teachers bully me and the boys in my class don't like me. Why?'

'Firstly, you're 35 years old,' replied his mother, 'and secondly, you're the principal!'

123 **T**eacher, teacher! I need a hanky.

Snot possible.

124 **T**eacher: *'Are you good at arithmetic?'*
Mary: *'Well, yes and no.'*
Teacher: *'What do you mean, yes and no?'*
Mary: *'Yes, I'm no good at arithmetic.'*

125 **T**eacher: *'If you had one dollar and asked your dad for one dollar, how much money would you have?'*

Student: *'One dollar.'*

Teacher: *'You don't know your maths.'*

Student: *'You don't know my dad!'*

126 **'B**e sure to go straight home from school.'

'I can't – I live around the corner!'

Animal Crackers

127 What time is it when an elephant climbs into your bed?

Time to get a new bed.

128 What do you get if you pour hot water down a rabbit hole?

Hot cross bunnies.

129 Why do buffaloes always travel in herds?

Because they're afraid of getting mugged by elephants.

130 What do you give a sick elephant?

A very big paper bag.

131 **W**here do elephants go on holidays?

Tuscany.

132 **W**hy are elephants big and grey?

Because if they were small and purple they would be grapes.

133 **W**hat do you call the red stuff between an elephant's toes?

A slow explorer.

134 **W**hy do elephants have Big Ears?

Because Noddy wouldn't pay the ransom.

135 **D**id you hear about the blind skunk?

He fell in love with a fart.

136 **W**here would you find a dog with no legs?

Exactly where you left it.

137 **W**hat did the buffalo say to his son, when he went away on a long trip?

'Bison.'

138 '**D**oes your dog bite?'

'No.'

'Oww. I thought you said your dog doesn't bite.'

'That's not my dog.'

139 **N**ame an animal that lives in Lapland.

A reindeer.

Now name another.

Another reindeer.

140 **W**hat sits in the middle of the World Wide Web?

A very, very big spider.

141 **W**hat animal always vomits after lunch?

A yak.

142 **C**ow 1: 'Are you concerned about catching mad cow disease?'

Cow 2: *'Not at all. I'm a sheep.'*

143 **W**hat does a cow's fart smell like?

Dairy air.

144 **H**ow did the frog die?

It Kermit-ted suicide.

145 **D**o you know where to find elephants?

Elephants don't need finding – they're so big they don't get lost.

146 **D**id you hear about the cannibal lioness?

She swallowed her pride.

BURRPP

OH PARDON ME!
Some of my friends obviously
don't agree with me!

147 **W**hat is a polygon?

A dead parrot.

148 **W**hat's the difference between a mouse and an elephant?

About a tonne.

149 **W**hat did the lioness say to the cub chasing the hunter?

Stop playing with your food.

Is that the
CODFATHER?

Yep...sure is!
What a nasty
piece of fish.

150 **W**hat do you get when you cross a master criminal with a fish?

The Codfather.

151   **W**hat do you get when you cross a baby rabbit with a vegetable?

A bunion.

152   **A** grizzly bear walks into a bar and says to the bartender, 'I'll have a gin and . . . tonic.'

Bartender: *'What's with the big pause?'*

Bear: *'I don't know. My father had them, too.'*

153   **W**hy did the man cross a chicken with an octopus?

So everyone in his family could have a leg each.

154   **W**hat is white, lives in the Himalayas and lays eggs?

The Abominable Snow Chicken.

155 **H**ow do pigs get clean?

They go to the hogwash.

156 **W**hat happens when a chimpanzee sprains his ankle?

He gets a monkey wrench.

157 **W**hat happened to two frogs that caught the same bug at the same time?

They got tongue-tied.

158 **H**ow do you know when it's raining cats and dogs?

You step into a poodle.

159 **W**hy did the dinosaur cross the road?

Because there were no chickens.

Where does a dinosaur cross a busy 6 Lane motorway? Anywhere it likes!!

160 **W**hat do you call a crazy chicken?

A cuckoo cluck.

161 **W**hat do you get if you cross Bambi with a ghost?

Bamboo.

162 **W**hy did the dinosaur not cross the road?

It was extinct.

163 **H**ow do cows count?

They use a cowculator.

164 **H**ow do you know when there is an elephant in the fridge?

There are footprints in the butter.

165 **W**hat's grey and can't see well from either end?

A donkey with its eyes shut.

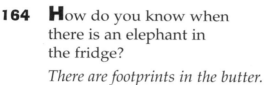

166 **W**hy are old dinosaur bones kept in a museum?

Because they can't find any new ones.

167 **W**hat's got six legs and can fly long distances?

Three swallows.

168 **W**hat do you get if you cross a pig with a zebra?

Striped sausages.

169 **D**id you hear about the monkey who left bits of his lunch all over the computer?

His dad went bananas.

170 **W**hat do you get if you cross a dinosaur with a werewolf?

Who knows, but I wouldn't want to be within a thousand miles of it when the moon is full!

171 **W**hy did the cat sit on the computer?

To keep an eye on the mouse.

172 **W**hen do kangaroos celebrate their birthdays?

During leap year.

173 **W**hat do baby swans dance to?

Cygnet-ure tunes.

174 **W**hat is a duck's favourite TV show?

The feather forecast.

175 **W**hat did the rabbit give his girlfriend when they got engaged?

A 24-carrot ring.

176 **W**hy don't baby birds smile?

Would you smile if your mother fed you worms all day?

177 **W**hat do you call a chicken that lays light bulbs?

A battery hen.

178 **W**hy do bears have fur coats?

Because they can't get plastic raincoats in their size!

179 **W**here is the hottest place in the jungle?

Under a gorilla.

180 **W**hat would you get if you crossed a hunting dog with a journalist?

A news hound.

181 **W**hat do you get if you cross a parrot with a shark?

A bird that will talk your ear off!

182 **D**octor, Doctor, I feel like a sheep.

That's baaaaaaaaaad!

183 **W**hat do you get if you cross an electric eel with a sponge?

Shock absorbers.

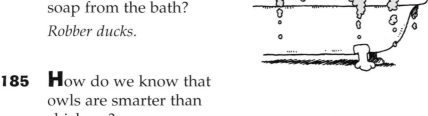

184 **W**hich birds steal the soap from the bath?

Robber ducks.

185 **H**ow do we know that owls are smarter than chickens?

Have you ever heard of Kentucky-fried owl?

186 **W**hen is a lion not a lion?

When he turns into his den.

187 **D**octor, Doctor, I think I'm a python.

You can't get round me just like that, you know!

188 **W**hat does an octopus wear when it's cold?

A coat of arms.

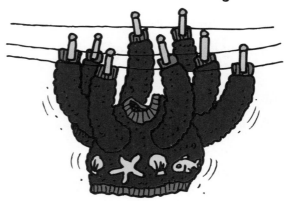

WASH DAY AT THE OCTOPUS' PLACE

189 **W**hat's slimy, tastes of raspberry, is wobbly and lives in the sea?

A red jellyfish.

190 **H**ow do you know when a spider is cool?

It has its own website.

191 **N**ow you see it, now you don't. What could you be looking at?

A black cat walking over a zebra crossing!

192 **W**hat did the mouse say to the elephant?

Squeak.

AAARHH

SQUEAK

193 **W**hat bird tastes just like butter?

A stork.

194 **W**hat's the difference between a dark sky and an injured lion?

One pours with rain, the other roars with pain.

195 **W**hat did the croaking frog say to her friend?

I think I've got a person in my throat.

196 **W**hat did the termite say when she saw that her friends had completely eaten a chair?

'Wooden you know it!'

197 **S**heep 1: *'Baa.'*

Sheep 2: *'I knew you were going to say that.'*

198 **W**hat are teenage giraffes told when they go on their first date?

No necking.

199 **W**hat did the boa constrictor say to its victim?

'I've got a crush on you.'

200 **W**hat disease do you have if you're allergic to horses?

Bronco-itis.

201 **W**hat do cats eat as a special treat?

Mice creams.

202 **W**hat do bees do with their honey?

They cell it.

203 **W**hat do bees use to communicate with each other?

Their cell phones.

204 **H**ow would you feel if you saw a dinosaur in your backyard?

Very old.

205 **W**hen did the last dinosaur die?

After the second-last dinosaur.

206 **W**hat do you cut a dinosaur bone with?

A dino-saw.

207 What do you get when you cross a dinosaur with a pig?

Jurassic Pork.

208 **W**hat do cows listen to?

Moosic.

209 **W**hat do you call a baby whale that never stops crying?

A little blubber.

210 **W**hat do you call a camel with no humps?

A horse.

211 **W**hy do elephants never get rich?

Because they work for peanuts.

212 **W**hat did the 100 kilo parrot say?

'Polly want a cracker, NOW!'

213 **D**id you hear about the duck decorator?

He papered over the quacks.

214 **W**hat did one bee say to her nosy neighbour bee?

'Mind your own bees' nest!'

215 **W**hat do you do with a mouse that squeaks?

You oil him.

216 **H**ow does a jellyfish race start?

Get set.

217 **W**hat do you call a cat who lives in a hospital?

A first aid kit.

218 **W**hat do you call a Chinese cat that spies through windows?

A Peking Tom.

219 **W**hat do you get when you cross a bear with a cow?

Winnie the Moo.

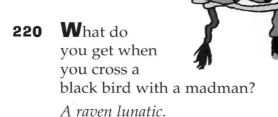

220 **W**hat do you get when you cross a black bird with a madman?

A raven lunatic.

221 **W**hat do you get when you cross a chicken with a cement mixer?

A bricklayer.

222 **W**hat do you get when you cross a cow with a clairvoyant?

A message from the udder side.

223 **W**hat do you get when you cross a shark with a crocodile and a Tyrannosaurus rex?

I don't know, but don't take it swimming.

224 **W**hat do you get when you cross a cow with a whale?

Mooby Dick.

225 **W**hat do you get if you cross a duck with a firework?

A fire-quacker.

226 **W**hat do you get when you cross a hare with a walking stick?

A hurry-cane (hurricane).

227 **W**hat do you get when you cross a kangaroo with a skyscraper?

A high jumper.

228 **W**hat do you get when you cross a mouse and a deer?

Mickey Moose.

229 **W**hat do you get when you cross a hippopotamus with someone who is always sick?

A hippochondriac.

230 **W**hat do you get when you cross a seagull with a pair of wheels?

A bi-seagull.

231 **W**hat do you get when you cross a sheep with a radiator?

Central bleating.

232 **W**hat do you get when you cross an elephant with a bottle of rum?

Trunk and disorderly.

233 **W**hat do you get when you cross an elephant with a cake?

Crumbs.

234 **W**hat language do birds speak?

Pigeon English.

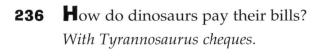

Someone suggested a game of 'HERE COMES THE LION' at Jumbo's 3rd Birthday party startling his 2 ton friends into a stampede.

235 **W**hat's as large as a horse but doesn't weigh anything?

Its shadow.

236 **H**ow do dinosaurs pay their bills?

With Tyrannosaurus cheques.

237 **H**ow do dinosaurs pass exams?

With extinction.

238 **W**hat do you get when you cross a dinosaur with explosives?

Dino-mite.

239 **W**hat do you get when you cross a Stegosaurus with a pig?

A porky spine.

240 **W**hat's the hardest part of making dinosaur stew?

Finding a pot big enough to hold the dinosaur.

241 **W**hat's the scariest dinosaur of all?

The Terrordactyl.

242 **W**here do dinosaurs go to the toilet?

In the dino-sewer.

SCARY HEY?

The scariest thing in Prehistoric skies...
The Terrorsaurus

243 **W**hich dinosaur does well in English exams?

Tyrannathesaurus rex.

244 **H**ow did Noah steer the Ark at night?

He switched on the floodlights.

After 40 days and 40 nights in this Ark with all these smelly animals... that looks like great land to me... THROW OUT THE ANCHOR!

245 **W**hy did the zookeeper refuse to work in the elephant enclosure?

Because the work kept piling up.

246 **W**hy do chickens watch TV?

For hentertainment.

247 **W**hy do frogs like beer?

Because it is made from hops.

248 **W**hat did Noah say as he was loading the animals?

'Now I herd everything.'

249 **W**hy don't cats shave?

Because they prefer Whiskas.

250 **W**hy is the letter 'T' important to a stick insect?

Because without it, it would be a sick insect.

251 **W**hy should you never fight an echidna?

Because she will always win on points.

252 **W**hy was the alligator called Kodak?

Because he was always snapping.

253 **W**hy did the chicken cross the road, roll in the mud and cross the road again?

Because it was a dirty double-crosser.

254 **W**hy did the chicken join the band?

Because it had drumsticks.

255 **W**hy did the fish cross the sea?

To get to the other tide.

256 **W**hy was the kangaroo mad at her children?

Because they were jumping on the bed.

257 **W**hy was the little bear spoilt?

Because he was panda'd to.

258 **W**hat do you get if you cross an elephant with a box of laxatives?

Out of the way.

259 **W**hy are dolphins clever?

Because they live in schools.

260 **W**hy can't frogs get life insurance?

Because they are always croaking.

261 **W**hy can't you have a conversation with a goat?
Because it always butts in.

262 **W**hich movie character do insects like best?
Bug Lightyear.

263 **W**hy are beavers so smart?
Because they gnaw everything.

264 **W**ho is the most feared animal of all?
Attila the Hen.

265 **W**hich TV show do cows never miss?
The moos.

266 **W**hich TV show do horses like best?
Neigh-bours.

267 **W**ho is emperor of all mice?
Julius Cheeser.

268 **W**ho is the king of the monkeys?
Henry the Ape.

269 **W**hy can't you play a practical joke on snakes?

Because they don't have a leg to pull.

270 **W**here would you weigh a whale?

At a whale-weigh station.

271 **W**hich animals are best at maths?

Rabbits, because they're always multiplying.

YAKKITY YAK...YAKKITY YAKKITTY YAKKITY YAKKITY YAK... Did you hear the joke about the yak that couldn't stop YAKKING? YAKK YAKK

Why YAKS are found only in the highest mountains of the Himalayas!

WOH THERE! A MINOR BIRD! I nearly stood on the little guy!

272 **W**hich animal never stops talking?

The yak.

273 **W**hich bird can lift the heaviest weights?

The crane.

274 **W**hich bird never grows up?

The minor bird.

275 **W**hich bird succeeds?

A budgie without teeth.

276 **W**hich hen lays the longest?

A dead one.

277 **W**hat do you give an elephant with diarrhoea?
Plenty of room.

278 **W**hat's the difference between a bird and a fly?
A bird can fly but a fly can't bird.

279 **W**hat's the difference between a buffalo and a bison?
You can't wash your hands in a buffalo.

280 **W**hat's the healthiest insect?
A vitamin bee.

281 **W**hen is a brown dog not a brown dog?
When it's a greyhound.

282 **W**hen is the best time to buy a canary?
When it's going cheap.

283 **W**here did the cow go for its holiday?

Moo Zealand.

284 **W**here do baby elephants come from?

Very big storks.

285 **W**here do baby monkeys sleep?

In an apricot.

286 **W**here do chickens go to die?

To oven.

287 **W**here did Noah keep the bees?

In the ark hives.

288 **W**here do cows go for entertainment?

The moovies.

289 **W**here do monkeys cook their dinner?

Under the gorilla.

Food for Thought

290 What can you serve, but never eat?

A tennis ball.

291 What vegetable goes well with jacket potatoes?

Button mushrooms.

292 What is a monster's favourite spread?

Toe jam.

293 What did the snowman say about the carrot cake?

Tastes like boogers.

294 **W**hat do you get when you cross an orange with a squash court?

Orange squash.

295 **W**hat happened when there was a fight in the fish and chip shop?

Two fish got battered.

296 **W**hy did the German spew after eating a sausage?

It brought out the wurst in him.

297 **W**hat did one tomato say to the other that was behind?

Ketchup!

Where all the slow tomatoes end up.

TOMATO KETCHUP

298 **W**hat is the difference between a hungry person and a greedy person?

One longs to eat, and the other eats too long.

299 **W**hat do bees do if they want to catch public transport?

Wait at a buzz stop.

300 **W**hat is the difference between broccoli and boogers?

Kids don't like to eat broccoli!

301 **W**hat's green and short and goes camping?

A boy sprout.

302 **H**ow do you make a bubble bath?

Eat baked beans for dinner.

303 **W**hy did the farmer plough his field with a steamroller?

He wanted to grow mashed potatoes.

304 **W**hy can't you order a booger in a restaurant?

Because it's snot on the menu.

305 **W**hat should you take if a monster invites you to dinner?

Someone who can't run as fast as you.

306 **W**hat did the dragon say when he saw St George in his shining armour?

'Oh no! Not more tinned food!'

307 **W**hen the cannibal crossed the Pacific on a cruise ship, he told the waiter to take the menu away and bring him the passenger list!

308 **W**here do ants eat?

A restaur-ant.

309 **W**hat do you do if your chicken feels sick?

Give her an eggs-ray.

310 **W**hat happened when the boy went to the bathroom and took a poo?

No one wanted it back so he got to keep it.

311 **M**other: *'I told you not to eat cake before supper.'*

Son: *'But it's part of my homework – see – if you take an eighth of a cake from a whole cake, how much is left?'*

312 **L**ucy: *'If you eat any more ice cream, you'll burst.'*

Lindy: *'Okay – pass the ice cream and duck.'*

313 **W**hat does a Yeti eat for dinner?

An ice-burger.

314 **K**nock knock.
Who's there?
Bach!
Bach who?
Bach of chips!

315 **K**nock knock.

Who's there?

Bacon!

Bacon who?

Bacon a cake for your birthday!

316 **A** man went into a cafe and ordered two slices of apple pie with four scoops of ice cream, covered with lashings of raspberry sauce and piles of chopped nuts.

'Would you like a cherry on top?' asked the waitress.

'No thanks,' said the man. *'I'm on a diet.'*

317 **W**hat do vultures always have for dinner?

Leftovers.

318 **H**ow do you make a cream puff?

Make it run around the block.

319 **W**hat's a monster's favourite chocolate?

Bellybutton Lindt.

320 **W**hy did the lazy boy get a job in a bakery?

Because he wanted a good loaf!

321 **K**nock knock.

Who's there?

Beef!

Beef who?

Bee fair now!

322 **D**octor, Doctor, I keep getting a pain in the eye when I drink coffee.

Have you tried taking the spoon out of the cup before you drink?

323 **K**nock knock.

Who's there?

Brie!

Brie who?

Brie me my supper!

324 **K**nock knock.

Who's there?

Butcher!

Butcher who?

Butcher arms around me!

325 **H**ave you ever seen a man-eating tiger?

No, but in a restaurant next door I once saw a man eating chicken . . .

326 **W**aiter, how did this fly get in my soup?

I guess it flew.

Boy! I hope I like this soup as much as these flies do!

327 **W**aiter, I can't eat this meal. Fetch me the manager.

It's no use. He won't eat it either.

328 **W**aiter, do you have frogs' legs?

Yes sir.

Then hop to the kitchen and fetch me a steak.

Gee... I'm glad I always carry a spare sausage behind my ear to write with.

329 **W**hen the silly man's co-worker asked why he had a sausage stuck behind his ear, he replied, '*Oh – I must have eaten my pencil for lunch!*'

330 **H**ow do you make a banana split?

Cut it in half.

331 **H**ow do you make a French fry?

Leave him in the sun.

332 **W**hat is the snotty kid's favourite restaurant?

Booger King.

My left thumb thinks it's Cream of Chicken ...my right thinks it's Pumpkin!

333 **'Y**our finger is in my bowl of soup!* said the man.

'Don't worry,' said the silly waiter. *'The soup isn't hot.'*

334 **W**hat happened to the male bee who fell in love?

He got stuck on his honey.

335 **W**hat's the best way to face a timid mouse?

Lie down in front of its mouse hole and cover your nose with cheese spread!

336 **W**here do sharks shop?

The fish market.

337 **W**hat do fishermen eat at Easter?

Oyster eggs.

338 **W**hat's a lawyer's favourite dessert?

Suet.

339 **W**hat's rhubarb?

Embarrassed celery.

340 **D**octor, Doctor, should I surf the Internet on an empty stomach?

No, you should do it on a computer.

341 **H**ow do you start a race between two rice puddings?

Sago.

342 **W**hat did the mayonnaise say to the fridge?

'Close the door, I'm dressing.'

343 **D**octor, Doctor, I feel like an apple.

We must get to the core of this!

Look..! NO CAKE!

344 **'W**illiam,' shouted his mum. *'There were two pieces of cake in that pantry last night, and now there's only one. How do you explain that?'*

'It was dark in the pantry,' said William. *'And I didn't see the second piece!'*

345 **W**aiter there's a fly in my soup.

Well you did order fly soup, ma'am.

346 **W**aiter, what kind of soup is this?

Bean soup.

I don't care what it's been. What is it now?

Is it any wonder I'm a SOURPUSS... That's not lemonade! That's VINEGAR!

347 **C**harley: *'My cat likes to drink lemonade.'*

Lenny: *'Golly, he sure must be a sourpuss!'*

348 **D**ick and Jane were arguing over the breakfast table.

'Oh, you're so stupid!' shouted Dick.

'Dick!' said their father. *'That's quite enough! Now say you're sorry.'*

'Okay,' said Dick. *'Jane, I'm sorry you're stupid.'*

349 Johnny collected lots of money from trick-or-treating and he went to the store to buy some chocolate.

'You should give that money to charity,' said the shopkeeper.

'No thanks,' replied Johnny. *'I'll buy the chocolate – you give the money to charity!'*

350 What kind of sharks never eat women?

Man-eating sharks.

351 How do you make a swiss roll?

Push him down a hill.

352 How do you make an apple crumble?

Smash it with a mallet.

353 Two cannibals were having lunch.

'Your girlfriend makes a great soup,' said one to the other.

'Yes!' agreed the first. *'But I'm going to miss her!'*

354 **H**ow do you make an egg laugh?

Tell it a yolk.

355 **W**hy did the girl feed money to her cow?

Because she wanted to get rich milk.

356 **W**hy did the girl put a chicken in a tub of hot water?

Because she wanted the chicken to lay hard-boiled eggs!

357 *'It's a pity you've gone on a hunger strike,'* said the convict's girlfriend on visiting day.

'Why?' asked the convict.

'Because I've put a file in your cake!'

Oh come on... I can handle a hair...or even half a cockroach in a cake... but not a FILE!

358 **G**irl: *'How much is a soft drink?'*
Waitress: *'Fifty cents.'*
Girl: *'How much is a refill?'*
Waitress: *'The first is free.'*
Girl: *'Well then, I'll have a refill.'*

359 **K**nock knock.
Who's there?
Cantaloupe!
Cantaloupe who?
Cantaloupe with you tonight!

360 **W**hat do you call an egg in the jungle?

An eggsplorer.

361 **K**nock knock.

Who's there?

Zubin!

Zubin who?

Zubin eating garlic again!

362 **A**my: *'Did you find your cat?'*

Karen: *'Yes, he was in the refrigerator.'*

Amy: *'Goodness, is he okay?'*

Karen: *'He's more than okay – he's a cool cat!'*

363 **W**aiter, I'd like burnt steak and soggy chips with a grimy, bitter salad.

I'm afraid the chef won't cook that for you, sir.

Why not? He did yesterday.

364 **W**hich cheese is made backwards?

Edam.

365 **W**hat vegetable can you play snooker with?

A cue-cumber.

366 **H**ow does Dracula eat his food?

In bite sized pieces.

367 **T**he cruise-ship passenger was feeling really seasick, when the waiter asked if he'd like some lunch.

'No thanks,' he replied. 'Just throw it over the side and save me the trouble.'

368 **W**hat's small, round, white and giggles?

A tickled onion.

369 **B**oy: *Help! I cut my finger slicing cheese!*

Mum: *Son, I think you have grater issues.*

370 **W**hy did the tomato blush?

Because it saw the salad dressing.

371 **W**hat do lions say before they go out hunting for food?

Let us prey.

372 **W**hat's a lion's favourite food?

Baked beings.

373 **W**hy do gingerbread men wear trousers?

Because they have crummy legs.

374 **A** mushroom walks into a bar and says to the bartender, *'Get me a drink!'*

But the bartender refuses.

The mushroom says, *'Why not? I'm a fun-gi!'*

We don't serve fungus at this bar! Besides... you're dropping spores all over the counter!

375 **W**hy do watermelons get married?

Because they can't-elope.

On account of the high crime rate and being previously assaulted... the pack of peanuts opted for a quiet night in.

376 **W**hy does steak taste better in space?

Because it is meteor.

377 **W**hy don't nuts go out at night?

Because they don't want to be assaulted.

378 **W**hat do cannibals eat to freshen their breath?

Men toes.

379 **W**aiter, there's a cockroach in my soup.

Sorry sir, we're all out of flies.

380 **W**hat are monsters' favourite lunches?

Shepherd's pie and ploughman's lunch.

381 **H**ow does Frankenstein eat?

He bolts his food down.

382 **K**nock knock.

Who's there?

U-8!

U-8 who?

U-8 my lunch!

True Colours

383 **W**hat's green, covered in custard and sad?

Apple grumble.

384 **W**hat's red on the outside and green inside?

A dinosaur wearing red pyjamas.

385 **B**oy monster: *'You've got a face like a million dollars.'*
Girl monster: *'Have I really?'*
Boy monster: *'Sure, it's green and wrinkly!'*

386 **B**oy: *'Dad there's a black cat in the dining room!'*
Dad: *'That's okay son, black cats are lucky.'*
Son: *'This one is – he's eaten your dinner!'*

387 Three girls walked into a barber shop. Two had blonde hair and one had green hair. The barber asked the blondes, *'How did you get to be blonde?'*

'Oh, it's natural,' they replied.

The barber asked the other girl, *'How did your hair become green?'*

She replied – (now put your hand on your nose and rub up to your hair . . .)

388 What do you do with a blue monster?

Try to cheer him up a bit.

Obviously radical babies

389 Why do we dress baby girls in pink and baby boys in blue?

Because babies can't dress themselves.

390 Visitor: *'You're very quiet, Louise.'*

Louise: *'Well, my mum gave me a dollar not to say anything about your red nose.'*

391 What is red, sweet and bites people?

A jampire!

392 If everyone bought a white car, what would we have?

A white carnation.

393 'Is that the computer help line? Every time I log on to the Seven Dwarves website, my computer screen goes snow white . . .'

394 What do you get if you cross a teacher and a traffic warden?

Someone who gives you 500 double yellow lines for being late.

395 What's the tallest yellow flower in the world?

A giraffodil.

396 Why did the monster paint himself in rainbow coloured stripes?

He wanted to hide in a pencil case.

397 **W**hat's black and white and red all over?

A sunburned zebra.

398 **W**hat's green and hard?

A frog that lifts weights.

399 **W**hat's red and white?

Pink.

400 **W**ho steals from her grandma's house?

Little Red Robin Hood.

401 **W**hat colour is a hiccup?

Burple.

402 **W**hat's red, white and brown and travels faster than the speed of sound?

An astronaut's ham and tomato sandwich.

403 **W**hat's green and pecks on trees?

Woody Wood Pickle.

404 **W**hat don't zombies wear on boat trips?

Life jackets.

405 **W**hat's green and sings?

Elvis Parsley.

406 **W**hat's green and slimy and hangs from trees?

Giraffe boogie.

On this tour of the African Plain you need to keep your eyes peeled for lions in long grass... scorpions under rocks... stampeding elephants... herds of wild wildebeasts... and of course Giraffe boogie in trees!

407 **W**hat's yellow and square?

A tomato in disguise.

408 **K**nock knock.

Who's there?

Beezer.

Beezer who?

Beezer black and yellow and make honey.

409 **W**hat goes in pink and comes out blue?

A swimmer on a cold day!

410 **W**hat's black and white and rolls down a hill?

A penguin.

411 **W**hat's black and white and laughs?

The penguin who pushed the other one.

412 **W**hat's big and white and can't jump over a fence?

A fridge.

413 **W**hich king was purple and had many wives?

King Henry the Grape.

414 **W**hat's purple, 5000 years old and 400 kilometres long?

The Grape Wall of China.

415 **W**hat's grey, has four legs and a trunk?

A mouse going on holiday.

Whatever possessed me to drag a heavy trunk around the world? I should have settled for a soft vinyl overnight bag with a zipper!

416 **W**hat's thick and black and picks its nose?

Crude oil.

417 **H**ow many clothing shop assistants does it take to change a light bulb?

Three, one to change it, one to say how well it fits and one to say that the colour is perfect.

Rude and Crude

418 **Y**ou're such a bad cook, even the maggots get takeaway.

419 **Y**our family is so weird, when the doorbell rings your sister has to shout out 'Ding, dong.'

420 **Y**ou are as useless as a screen door on a submarine.

421 **W**ith you here, your village must be missing its idiot.

Come back here little fella...; Don't go wandering off... you're the only mind I've got!

422 **D**on't let your mind wander – it's too little to be let out alone.

423 **S**tatistics say that one in three people is wacky.

So check your friends and if two of them seem okay, you're the one . . .

424 **W**hat do you call a banker who has no friends?

A loaner.

425 **W**hat do you get when royalty farts?

A noble gas.

426 **T**urn the other cheek. On second thoughts, don't. The view is just as ugly on that side.

427 You're not as stupid as you look. That would be impossible.

428 I'd leave you with one thought if you had somewhere to put it.

429 Your feet are so smelly, your shoes refuse to come out of the closet.

The other shoes in the wardrobe could stand the smell no longer... so the stinky sandshoes were shown the door...

430 If it's true that opposites attract, you'll meet someone who is good-looking, intelligent and cultured.

431 Everyone has the right to be ugly, but you abused the privilege.

432 She's so ugly, when a wasp stings her, it has to shut its eyes!

I'm not that desperate to sting someone!

433 If someone offered you a penny for your thoughts, they'd expect some change.

434 You're dark and handsome. When it's dark, you're handsome.

435 Last time I saw someone as ugly as you, I had to pay admission.

436 As an outsider, what do you think of the human race?

437 Instead of drinking from the fountain of knowledge, you just gargled.

438 They say that truth is stranger than fiction. And you're the proof.

439 I'll never forget the first time we met – although I keep trying.

440 Someone told me you're not fit to live with pigs but I stuck up for you and said you were.

441 You're so boring, you won't even talk to yourself.

442 You're so ugly, the only dates you get are on a calendar.

443 You're so ugly you have to trick or treat over the phone.

444 Are poop jokes everyone's favourite?
No, but they're a solid Number Two.

445 '**D**addy, can I have another glass of water, please?'

'Okay, but that's the twelfth one I've given you tonight.'

'Yes I know, but the house is still on fire.'

446 '**G**randma: *'I've just done a silent fart and it might be stinky. What should I do?'*

Grandad: *'Replace the batteries in your hearing aid.'*

447 **G**eorge is the type of boy that his mother doesn't want him to hang around with . . .

448 **W**hat's worse than biting your fingernails?

Biting your toenails.

449 **A** woman woke her husband in the middle of the night.

'There's a burglar in the kitchen eating the cake I made this morning!' she said.

'Who should I call?' asked her husband. *'The police or an ambulance?'*

450 **M**y cousin spent heaps on deodorant, until he found out people just didn't like him . . .

451 **D**id you hear about the two bodies cremated at the same time?

It was a dead heat.

452 **H**ave you seen the movie `Constipated'?

It hasn't come out yet.

453 **H**ave you seen the sequel 'Diarrhoea'?

It leaked so they had to release it.

454 **W**hy shouldn't you fart in an Apple store?

They don't have Windows.

455 Three guys, Shutup, Manners and Poop, drove too fast and Poop fell out of the car.

Shutup went to the police station, where the policeman asked, *'What's your name?'*

'Shutup,' he answered.

'Hey – where are your manners!' the policeman exclaimed.

Shutup replied, *'Outside on the road, scrapin' up Poop!'*

456 As he was walking along a street, the minister saw a little girl trying to reach a high door knocker. Anxious to help, he went over to her. *'Let me do it, dear,'* he said, rapping the knocker.

'Thanks,' said the little girl. *'Now run like heck!'*

457 Why did the female frog lay eggs?

Because her husband spawned her affections.

458 Uncle Herbert noticed that his nephew Johnny was watching him all the time.

'Why are you always looking at me?' he asked.

'I was just wondering when you were going to do your trick,' replied Johnny.

'What trick?' asked Uncle Herbert.

'Well, Mum says you eat like a horse...'

459 **A** man out for a walk came across a little boy pulling his cat's tail.

'Hey you!' he shouted. *'Don't pull the cat's tail!'*

'I'm not pulling,' replied the boy. *'I'm only holding on – the cat's doing the pulling. . .'*

460 **W**hy did the toilet feel upset?

Because everybody kept dumping on it.

461 **W**hat did Steve Jobs say when he let off gas?

iFarted.

462 **W**hen the man was run over by a steamroller, what was proved?

That he had lots of guts.

The next scene is just too ugly to draw . . .'

463 **W**hy is diarrhoea hereditary?

It runs in your jeans.

464 **W**hy doesn't Taylor Swift wipe after pooping?

She just shakes it off.

465 **Y**ou're growing on me – like a wart.

466 **N**ever criticise someone until you have walked a mile in their shoes.

That way, when you criticise them, you'll be a mile away, and you'll have their shoes.

467 **W**hy do only four out of every five people suffer from flatulence?

Because the other one enjoys it.

World of Sport

468 **W**hat has 75 pairs of sneakers, a ball and two hoops?

A centipede basketball team.

469 **W**hy didn't the silly goalkeeper catch the ball?

He thought that's what the net was for.

'Hey... you'll have to do that again ... I wasn't ready.'

470 **'I** can't see us ever finishing this tenpin bowling game.'

'Why is that?'

'Every time I knock all the pins down, someone calls everyone out on strike!'

I don't know how many soccer players it takes to change a lightbulb... but whoever kicked the ball can change it.

471 **H**ow many soccer players does it take to change a light bulb?

Eleven, one to change it, the others to jump about, hugging and kissing him.

472 **W**hy aren't football stadiums built in outer space?

Because there is no atmosphere!

473 **W**hich goalkeeper can jump higher than a crossbar?

All of them – a crossbar can't jump!

Get real! Who do we think we're fooling! How are we going to pass for baby swans when we look like a herd of dancing pigs in tu-tus!

474 **W**hat's a pig's favourite ballet?

Swine Lake.

475 **W**here do footballers dance?

At a football!

476 **W**hy did the golfer wear two pairs of trousers?

In case he got a hole in one.

477 **W**hat job does Dracula have with the Transylvanian baseball team?

He looks after the bats.

478 **W**hat do you call a cat that plays football?

Puss in boots.

479 **W**hat did the punter say when he pulled out a huge booger?

I picked a winner!

480 **W**hy do football coaches bring suitcases along to away games?

So that they can pack the defence!

481 If you have a referee in football, what do you have in bowls?

Cornflakes!

482 How do hens encourage their football teams?

They egg them on!

483 How do you start a doll's race?

Ready, Teddy, Go!

484 Who won the race between two balls of string?

They were tied!

485 How did the basketball court get wet?

The players dribbled all over it!

486 Why don't grasshoppers go to football matches?

They prefer cricket matches!

487 Why didn't the dog want to play football?

It was a boxer!

488 **W**hen fish play football, who is the captain?

The team's kipper!

489 **H**ow do you stop squirrels playing football in the garden?

Hide the ball, it drives them nuts!

490 **W**hy should you be careful when playing against a team of big cats?

They might be cheetahs!

491 **N**ame a tennis player's favourite city.

Volley Wood!

492 **W**here do football directors go when they are sick of the game?

The bored room!

493 **W**hat's a vampire's favourite sport?

Batminton.

494 **W**hat do vampire footballers have at half time?

Blood oranges.

495 **C**oach: *'I thought I told you to lose weight. What happened to your three-week diet?'*

Player: *'I finished it in three days!'*

496 **W**hat do you get when you cross a skunk with a table-tennis ball?

Ping pong.

497 **H**ow many baseball players does it take to change a light bulb?

Two, one to change it, the other to signal which way to do it.

498 **W**hat do you get when you cross a plumber with a ballerina?

A tap dancer.

499 **C**oach: *'Our new player cost ten million. I call him our wonder player.'*

Fan: *'Why's that?'*

Coach: *'Every time he plays, I wonder why I bothered to buy him!'*

500 **C**oach: *'I'll give you $100 a week to start with, and $500 a week in a year's time.'*

Young player: *'See you in a year!'*

501 **W**hat did the football player say when he accidentally burped during the game?

'Sorry, it was a freak hic!'

502 **W**hat part of a basketball stadium is never the same?

The changing rooms!

503 **W**hy did the diver poop before the tryouts?

He wanted to make a splash.

504 **W**here do old bowling balls end up?

In the gutter!

505 **W**hy do artists never win when they play basketball?

They keep drawing!

506 **W**hat are Brazilian fanatics called?

Brazil nuts!

507 **W**hy didn't the booger make the basketball team?

It didn't get picked.

508 **W**hy does someone who runs marathons make a good student?

Because education pays off in the long run!

509 **W**hat stories are told by basketball players?

Tall stories!

510 **W**hy did the footballer take a piece of rope onto the pitch?

He was the skipper!

511 **W**hat baseball position did the boy with no arms or legs play?

Home base.

512 **W**hat wears nine gloves, 18 shoes and a mask?

A baseball team.

513 **W**hy was the struggling manager seen shaking the club cat?

To see if there was any money in the kitty!

Music to My Ears

514 **W**hy did the singer climb a ladder?

To reach the high notes.

515 **H**ow many country music singers does it take to change a light bulb?

Two, one to change it, the other to sing about how heartbroken he is that the old one is finished.

516 **D**id you hear about the silly burglar?

He robbed a music store and stole the lute.

517 **W**hat type of music do mummies like best?

Ragtime.

518 **W**hat's a skeleton's favourite musical instrument?

A trom-bone.

519 **'M**y brother's been practising the violin for ten years.'

'Is he any good?'

'No, it was nine years before he found out he wasn't supposed to blow!'

520 **K**nock knock.
Who's there?
Cecil.
Cecil who?
Cecil have music
wherever she goes.

521 **W**hat do you call
a guy who hangs
around musicians?
A drummer.

522 **W**hat type of music do zombies like best?
Soul music.

523 **W**hat sort of music is played most in the jungle?
Snake, rattle and roll.

524 **W**hat type of music do geologists like best?
Rock.

525 **W**hy did the
monster eat his
music teacher?
*His Bach was worse
than his bite.*

526 **W**hat was Pavarotti before he was a tenor?

A niner.

527 **W**hat do you call a small Indian guitar?

A baby sitar.

528 **W**here do musicians live?

In A flat.

529 **'T**his piece of music is haunting.'

'That's because you're murdering it.'

530 **H**ow do you make a bandstand?

Take away their chairs.

The painful murder of the "1812 Overture"

531 **'I** played Beethoven last night.'

'Who won?'

I dig that grooovy sole music!

532 **W**hy did the footballer hold his boot to his ear?

Because he liked sole music!

533 **'W**hat shall I sing next?'

'Do you know "Bridge Over Troubled Waters?"'

'Yes.'

'Then go and jump off it.'

534 **W**hat do Eskimos sing at birthday parties?

'Freeze a Jolly Good Fellow.'

535 **W**hat does a musician take to the supermarket?

A Chopin Lizst.

536 **'O**ur Jackie learnt to play the violin in no time at all.'

'So I can hear.'

537 **W**hat instrument does a fisherman play?

A cast-a-net.

538 **W**hy couldn't the composer be found?

Because he was Haydn.

539 **W**hy was the musician in prison?

Because he was always getting into treble.

540 **W**hat is the snot monster's favourite song?

Greensleeves.

541 **W**here do musical frogs perform?

At the Hopera House.

Dumb and Dumber

542 **Y**ou're so dumb, when you eat M&Ms, you throw out the Ws.

543 **Y**ou're so ugly, when you enter a room, the mice jump on chairs.

Yep...that's right... It's a new mobile phone that has enough cable to reach just about anywhere!

544 **Y**ou're so dumb, you took your mobile phone back to the shop because it came without a cord.

545 **Y**ou're so dumb, it takes you an hour to cook one-minute noodles.

546 You're so dumb, you think the English Channel is a British TV station.

547 Did you hear what Dumb Donald did when he offered to paint the garage for his dad?

The instructions said put on three coats – so he put on his jacket, his raincoat and his overcoat!

548 My girlfriend talks so much that when she goes on vacation, she has to spread suntan lotion on her tongue!

549 Little Susie stood in the department store near the escalator, watching the moving handrail.

'Something wrong, little girl?' asked the security guard.

'Nope,' replied Susie. *'I'm just waiting for my chewing gum to come back.'*

550 **E**mma: *'What a cool pair of odd socks you have on, Jill.'*
Jill: *'Yes, and I have another pair just like it at home.'*

551 **D**ad: *'Don't be selfish. Let your brother use the sled half the time.'*

Son: *'I do, Dad. I use it going down the hill and he gets to use it coming up the hill!'*

552 **W**hy did the lion feel sick after he'd eaten the priest?

Because it's hard to keep a good man down.

553 **Y**ou're so dumb, when you went to the mind reader they couldn't find anything to read.

554 **'D**ad, can you write in the dark?'

'*I suppose so.*'

'Good. Can you sign my report card, please?'

555 **'M**um, I'm not going to school today.'

'*Why not?*'

'Because it's Sunday.'

556 **M**y big brother is such an idiot. The other day I saw him hitting himself over the head with a hammer.

He was trying to make his head swell, so his hat wouldn't fall over his eyes!

An ILL-FITTING HAT? I've got the perfect solution for an ill-fitting hat!

557 **W**hy did Silly Sue throw her guitar away?

Because it had a hole in the middle.

558 **A** man whose son had just passed his driving test came home one evening and found that the boy had driven into the living room.

'*How did you manage that?*' he fumed.

'*Quite simple, Dad,*' said the boy. '*I just came in through the kitchen and turned left.*'

559 'Why are you crying, Ted?' asked his mum.

'Because my new sneakers hurt,' Ted replied.

'That's because you've put them on the wrong feet.'

'But they're the only feet I have!'

560 'Mum, Mum, Dad's broken my computer!'

'How did he do that?'

'I dropped it on his head!'

561 Did you hear about my brother?

He saw a moose's head hanging on a wall and went into the next room to find the rest of it!

562 A boy was staying in an old house, and in the middle of the night, he met a ghost.

'I've been walking these corridors for 300 years,' said the ghost.

'In that case, can you tell me where the bathroom is?' asked the boy.

563 First witch: *'I took my son to the zoo yesterday.'*
Second witch: *'Really? Did they keep him?'*

564 Did you hear about the constipated mathematician?
He worked it out with a pencil.

565 Did you hear about the constipated accountant?
He couldn't budget.

566 'Mum,' Richard yelled from the kitchen. *'You know that dish you were always worried I'd break?'*
'Yes dear, what about it?' said his mum.
'Well . . . your worries are over.'

567 'Mum, there's a man at the door collecting for the Old Folks' Home,' said the little boy. *'Shall I give him Grandma?'*

Mum won't be too mad....
It's only broken into 3 big bits.

568 Two girls were having lunch in the school yard. One had an apple, and the other said, *'Watch out for worms, won't you!'*
The first girl replied, *'Why should I? They can watch out for themselves!'*

569 **W**hat do you call a top girl-group made up of nits?

The Lice Girls!

570 **W**hy did the boy wear a life jacket in bed?

Because he slept on a waterbed.

571 **J**ane: *'Do you like me?'*

Wayne: *'As girls go, you're fine . . . and the sooner you go, the better!'*

572 **D**ad was taking Danny around the museum, when they came across a magnificent stuffed lion in a case.

'Dad,' asked a puzzled Danny. *'How did they shoot the lion without breaking the glass?'*

573 Boy: *'Grandpa, do you know how to croak?'*

Grandpa: *'No, I don't. Why?'*

Boy: *'Because Daddy says he'll be a rich man when you do!'*

574 You're so slow, you can't even catch your breath.

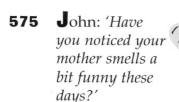

575 John: *'Have you noticed your mother smells a bit funny these days?'*

Will: *'No. Why?'*

John: *'Well, your sister told me she was giving her a bottle of toilet water for her birthday!'*

576 You're so dumb, when your teacher said she wanted you to get ahead, she really meant 'a head'.

577 *'Mum, can I please change my name right now?'* asked Ben.

'Why would you want to do that, dear?' asked his mum.

'Because Dad says he's going to spank me, as sure as my name's Benjamin!'

578 **W**hat does a
silly man pour
over his meat?

Thick gravy.

579 **G**eorge knocked on the door of his friend's house.
When his friend's mother answered he asked, *'Can
Albert come out to play?'*

'No,' said Albert's mother. *'It's too cold.'*

'Well then,' said George, *'can his football come out
to play?'*

580 **'W**illiam, I've been told you tried to put paint on
two boys at school,' said his dad.

'Yes Dad,' said William.

They're twins and I needed a way to tell them apart!'

581 **D**id you hear about the girl who was so keen on road safety that she always wore white at night?

Last winter she was knocked down by a snow plough.

582 **W**hat do young female monsters do at parties?

They go around looking for edible bachelors!

583 **O**ne day Joe's mother said to his father, *'It's such a nice day, I think I'll take Joe to the zoo.'*

'I wouldn't bother,' said his father. *'If they want him, let them come and get him!'*

584 Why did the silly team always lose the tug of war?

They pushed . . .

585 **D**id you hear about the silly man who went waterskiing?

He spent his whole holiday looking for a sloping lake.

Stand still yer lilly-livered layabouts so I can cut yez all into little pieces!

But you've got to play fair and tell me wherz ya are first.

586 **D**id you hear about the silly pirate?

He had a patch over both eyes.

587 **D**id you hear about the silly school kid who was studying Greek mythology?

When the teacher asked him to name something that was half-man and half-beast he replied, 'Buffalo Bill'.

588 **H**andsome Harry: *'Every time I walk past a girl, she sighs.'*

Wisecracking William: *'With relief!'*

589 **W**hy was the Egyptian girl worried?

Because her Daddy was a Mummy!

Ahhr... MR Mummy... SIR.. would it be OK to take your daughter on a date ...cruise the Nile... see some Pyramids?

590 **H**eard about the foolish karate champion who joined the army?

The first time he saluted, he nearly killed himself.

591 **T**he teacher told Sammy he knew he'd skipped school last Friday, and heard he'd been playing at the games arcade.

Sammy told him it wasn't true – and he had the football game tickets to prove it!

592 **R**obert saw a sign outside a police station that read: 'Man Wanted For Robbery,' so he went in and applied for the job!

593 **W**hy did the man get 17 of his friends to accompany him to the movies?

Because he'd heard it was not for under-18s.

594 **T**he gangland boss was surprised to find one of his gang sawing the legs off his bed.

'Why are you doing that?' he asked.

'Well, you did ask me to lie low for a bit,' the silly man replied.

595 **S**usie asked the silly man if his tent leaked when he was on holiday.

'Only when it rained,' he said.

596 **W**hy did the silly pilot land his plane on a house?

Because they'd left the landing lights on.

597 **'A**re you lost?' the policeman asked the silly schoolgirl.

'Of course not,' she replied. *'I'm here, it's my school that's lost.'*

598 **D**id you hear about the silly hitchhiker?

He got up early so there wouldn't be much traffic around.

599 **H**ave you heard about the man who went into an 'Open 24 hours a day' store and asked what time they closed?

600 **'D**o you turn on your computer with your left hand or your right hand?'

'My right hand.'

'Amazing! Most people have to use the on/off switch!'

601 **C**ustomer: 'I cleaned my computer and now it doesn't work.'

Repairman: *'What did you clean it with?'*

Customer: 'Soap and water.'

Repairman: *'Water's never meant to get near a computer!'*

Customer: 'Oh, I bet it wasn't the water that caused the problem . . . it was when I put it in the spin dryer!'

602 **H**ow do you milk a mouse?

You can't. The bucket won't fit under it.

603 How do you stop a dog doing his business in the hall?

Put him outside.

604 'I play Scrabble with my pet dog every night.'

'He must be clever.'

'I don't know about that. I usually beat him.'

Don't let Rex out darling... Just play ball with him... He's in for the day because it's raining....

RRRRR! Rex want to go out!

Rex doesn't care if it's raining!!! Rex need to go...NOW!

605 'I've lost my dog.'

'Put an ad in the paper.'

'Don't be silly. He can't read.'

606 What do you get when you cross a flower with a silly man?

A blooming idiot.

eeee...hee..hee... ooh...ooh...ahhrr

GREAT! A plant with a mental problem.'

607 A man went to the train station

Man: 'I'd like a return ticket please.'

Ticket seller: *'Certainly sir, where to?'*

'Back here of course.'

608 **H**ow many silly people does it take to change a light bulb?

Five, one to climb the ladder, the others to turn the ladder around and around.

609 **'W**hat's the weather like?'

'I don't know. It's too foggy to tell.'

610 **A** silly man was just about to dive into a pool when a lifesaver came rushing up.

Lifesaver: *'Don't jump. There's no water in the pool.'*

Man: *'It's okay. I can't swim.'*

611 **D**id you hear about the silly glass blower?

He inhaled and got a pane in the tummy.

612 **D**id you hear about the silly secretary?

She was so good she could type 60 mistakes a minute.

613 **D**id you hear about the silly shoe repairman?

A customer gave him a pair of shoes to be soled, so he sold them.

614 **D**id you hear about the silly man who had a brain transplant?

The brain rejected him.

615 **D**id you hear about the silly shoplifter?

He hurt his back trying to lift the corner store.

616 **D**id you hear about the other silly shoplifter?

He stole a free sample.

617 **D**id you hear about the silly photographer?

He saved used light bulbs for his dark room.

618 **W**hy did
the silly man
throw away his
doughnut?

*Because it had a
hole in the middle.*

619 **D**id you hear
about the silly
man who locked
his keys in the car?

He called a mechanic to get his family out.

620 **D**id you hear about the silly water polo
player?

His horse drowned.

621 **D**id you hear
about the silly
man who spent
two hours in a
department store?

*He was looking for
a cap with a peak at
the back.*

622 **D**id you hear about the silly man who stole a calendar?

He got 12 months.

623 **D**id you hear about the silly glazier who tried to fit a new window?

He broke it with a hammer.

624 **W**hat did the silly window cleaner have on the top of his ladder?

A stop sign.

What a ridiculous place for a STOP SIGN! What do they think I am...? A WALLY?

625 **D**id you hear about the silly man who wanted value for money?

He sat at the back of the bus to get a longer ride.

SISSSSS

Hello JIM'S IRONING SERVICE. We home deliver!

626 **D**id you hear about the silly man who went skiing?

He skied up the slope and caught the chair lift down.

627 **H**ow did the silly man burn his ear?

He was ironing when the phone rang.

628 **W**hat about the silly man who burnt both his ears?
The caller rang back.

629 **W**hy shouldn't you fart in church?
You have to sit in your own pew.

630 **H**ow much should a fart weigh?
Nothing. Any more and you're in trouble!

631 **D**id you hear about the boy who wanted to run
away to the circus?
He ended up in a flea circus!

632 **'W**hat's the difference between a marshmallow and a pykost?'

'What's a pykost?'

'About two dollars.'

633 **'M**ay I try on that dress in the window?'

'No. I'm afraid you'll have to use the dressing room like everyone else.'

Love Me Tender

634 **W**hat happened when the young wizard met the young witch?

It was love at first fright.

635 **W**hy is a bride always out of luck on her wedding day?

Because she never marries the best man.

636 **W**hat did the undertaker say to his girlfriend?

Em-balmy about you!

637 **D**id you hear about the vampire who died of a broken heart?

She had loved in vein.

638 **W**hat did the skeleton say to his girlfriend?

I love every bone in your body!

639 **W**hat feature do witches love on their computers?

The spell-checker.

640 **W**ho is a vampire likely to fall in love with?

The girl necks door.

641 **W**hat do girl snakes write on the bottom of their letters?

With love and hisses!

642 James: *'I call my girlfriend Peach.'*
John: *'Because she's soft, and beautiful as a peach?'*
James: *'No, because she's got a heart of stone.'*

643 **'I** got a gold watch for my girlfriend.'
'I wish I could make a trade like that!'

So what did you trade for that?

GRANDAD

644 Witch: *'When I'm old and ugly, will you still love me?'*
Wizard: *'I do, don't I?'*

645 **'D**o you think, Professor, that my girlfriend should take up the piano as a career?'
'No, I think she should put down the lid as a favour!'

Their marriage was doomed from the start...he wanted a cliffside wedding...she didn't...

646 What do you get when you cross a wedding with a cliff?
A marriage that is on the rocks.

647   First man: *'My girlfriend eats like a bird.'*
Second man: *'You mean she hardly eats a thing?'*
First man: *'No, she eats slugs and worms.'*

648   Did you hear about the monster who sent his picture to a lonely hearts club?
They sent it back, saying they weren't that lonely.

649   What does every kid have that they can always count on?
Fingers.

When you count to 10 using your fingers... Are you allowed to count your thumbs?

650   What happened when the snowman girl had a fight with her boyfriend?
She gave him the cold shoulder.

651 Every time I take my girlfriend out for a meal, she eats her head off.

She looks better that way.

652 What did the booger write in the Valentine's Day card?

I'd pick you first.

653 What did the wizard say to his witch girlfriend?

Hello, gore-juice!

654 When Wally Witherspoon proposed to his girlfriend, she said, *'I love the simple things in life, Wally, but I don't want one of them for a husband!'*

655 What did the bull say to the cow?

'I'll love you for heifer and heifer.'

656 What do you call a hippo that believes in peace, love and understanding?

A hippie-potamus.

657 Who were the world's shortest lovers?

Gnomeo and Juliet.

658 Knock knock.

Who's there?

Ida.

Ida who?

Ida know why I love you like I do.

659 I can't understand why people say my girlfriend's legs look like matchsticks.

They do look like sticks – but they certainly don't match!

660 What do you get when you cross a vampire with a computer?

Love at first byte.

What Do You Call...

661 **W**hat do you call a man who shaves 15 times a day?
A barber.

662 **W**hat do you call a dinosaur that never gives up?
A try and try and try-ceratops.

It takes 15 shaves a day to keep my face as smooth as this.
Oh...and a box of sticking plaster a bottle of antiseptic...and a good first aid kit...

663 **W**hat do you call an elephant that flies?

A jumbo jet.

664 **W**hat do you call a bee that buzzes quietly?

A mumble bee.

665 **W**hat do you call a cow that eats grass?

A lawn mooer.

666 **W**hat do you call a deer with only one eye?

No idea.

667 **W**hat do you call a deer with no legs and only one eye?

Still no idea.

668 **W**hat do arctic
cows live in?

An igmoo.

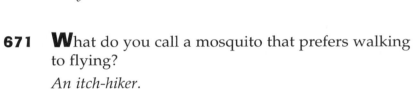

669 **W**hat do you call
a fish with no eyes?

Fsh.

670 **W**hat do you call
a messy cat?

Kitty litter.

671 **W**hat do you call a mosquito that prefers walking
to flying?

An itch-hiker.

672 **W**hat do you call a pig that does karate?

Pork chop.

673 **W**hat do you call a pig who enjoys jumping from a great height?

A stydiver.

674 **W**hat do you call a Russian fish?

A Tsardine.

675 **W**hat do you call an elephant that flies straight up?

An elecopter.

676 **W**hat do you call a pig with no clothes on?

Streaky bacon.

677 **W**hat do you call a well-behaved goose?

A propaganda.

678 **W**hat do you call a young goat who visits a psychiatrist?

A mixed-up kid.

679 **W**hat do you call a sheep in a bikini?

Bra-bra black sheep.

680 **W**hat do you call a shy sheep?

Baaaashful.

681 **W**hat do you call a tall building that pigs work in?

A styscraper.

682 **W**hat do you call a zebra without stripes?

A horse.

683 **W**hat do you call cattle that always sit down?

Ground beef.

684 **W**hat do you call the ghost of a chicken?

A poultrygeist.

685 **W**hat do you call two pigs who write letters to each other?

Pen-pals.

686 **W**hat do you call a man with a bus on his head?

Dead.

687 **W**hat do you call a bear with no fur?

A bare.

688 **W**hat do you call a
detective skeleton?

Sherlock Bones.

689 **W**hat do you call
a witch without a
broomstick?

A witch-hiker.

690 **W**hat do you call a
hairy beast in a river?

A weir-wolf.

691 **W**hat do you call
a skeleton who sits
around doing
nothing?

Lazy bones.

692 **W**hat do you call a protest march by devils?

A demon-stration.

693 **W**hat do you call banana skins that you wear on your feet?

Slippers.

694 **W**hat do you call two rows of vegetables?

A dual cabbageway.

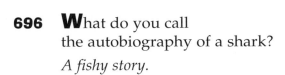

695 **W**hat do you call a flea who flies inside a silly man's head?

A space invader.

696 **W**hat do you call the autobiography of a shark?

A fishy story.

697 **W**hat do you call a dimwit with half a brain?

A genius.

698 **W**hat do you call a crate of ducks?

A box of quackers.

699 **W**hat do you call a neurotic octopus?

A crazy, mixed-up squid.

700 **W**hat do you call a bird that lives underground?

A mynah bird.

Definitely NOT a crate of ducks!

DANGER

701 **W**hat do you call a mouse that can pick up a monster?

Sir.

702 **W**hat do you call a man with a plank on his head?

Edward!

703 **W**hat do you call a woman with a toilet on her head?

Lu!

WATCH IT BIG BOY!

704 **W**hat do you call a woman with two toilets on her head?

Lulu!

705 **W**hat do you call a lion wearing a hat?

A dandy lion.

706 **W**hat do you call a crazy spaceman?

An astronut!

707 **W**hat do you call a space magician?

A flying sorcerer!

708 **W**hat do you call a robot who takes the longest route?

R2 Detour!

709 **W**hat do you call a monster who comes to collect your laundry?

An undie-taker.

710 **W**hat do you call a girl with a frog in her mouth?

Lily!

711 **W**hat do you call an old and foolish vampire?

A silly old sucker!

712 **W**hat do you call two witches who share a room?

Broom mates!

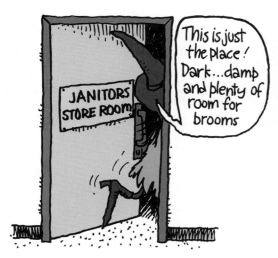

713 **W**hat do you call someone who doesn't have all their fingers on one hand?

Normal. You have fingers on both hands!

714 **W**hat do you call someone who greets you at the school door every morning?

Matt.

Fully Booked

George! Wake up! Did you hear that snoring noise? It sounds like someone sawing through our bedroom wall

Within minutes... the day at the beach became a swim in the ocean....

720 '**W**here Did That Go?' by Loz Tabogey

721 '**H**ousing Problem' by
Rufus Quick

722 '**K**eeping Warm at Night'
by Ida Down

723 '**F**irst He Farted'
by Denny Pood

724 '**S**top Making Me
Laugh!' by P de Little

725 '**T**he Sewerage Worker' by Hans R Brown

726 '**F**eeling Lighter' by Ida Bogg

727 'The Greediest Monster' by Buster Gutt

728 'Butt Orchestras' by I B Tootin

729 'Foaming at the Mouth' by Dee Monic

730 'Creature from Another World' by A Lee-En

Take me to your leader!

731 'I Saw a Witch' by Denise R Knockin

732 'In the Cannibal's Cauldron' by Mandy Ceased

733 'My Crystal Ball' by CA Lot

I see...

DISASTER

734 'I Met a Vampire' by Pearce Nex

735 'Smells Like Eggs' by Dee Lightful

736 'Making Money from Rich Wizards' by Marie Mee

737 'That Was Me!' by Yuri Welcome

749 **'T**ape Recording for Beginners' by Cass Ette

750 **'D**on't Leave Without Me' by Isa Coming

751 **'W**hen Shall We Meet Again?' by Miles Apart

752 'The Antarctic Ocean' by IC Waters

753 'Will He Win?' by Betty Wont

754 'Hair Disorders' by Dan Druff

755 'Showering Yearly' by Lon Lee Guy

756 'Pain and Sorrow' by Anne Guish

757 'Don't Touch Handrails' by Orla Stickey

758 'Crossing Roads Safely' by Luke Bothways

759 'The Laser Weapon' by Ray Gunn

760 'Fade Away' by Peter Out

761 'Facial Warts' by Aunt I Priddy

762 '**R**omantic Remembrance' by Valentine Card

763 '**E**ating Boogers' by Mae B Delicious

764 '**T**he Hungry Yeti' by Aida Lott

765 '**F**ollowing Through' by Ronnie Bottom

766 '**R**epairing Old Clothes' by Fred Bare

A poor millionaire

781 'The Garlic Eater' by I Malone

782 'Hosting a Party' by Maude D Merrier

783 'Bathroom Disaster!' by Don Taveny Paper

784 'Robbers Who Got Away With It' by Hugh Dunnit

PARTY PARTY PARTY

785 'Bless You!' by Hank E Green

786 'Keeping Pet Snakes' by Sir Pent

787 'Blasted Blister' by Ima Poppett

788 'Chin Hair' by Ima Pluckett

789 'Itchy Scab' by Ima Pickett

What happened to your pet guinea pig?

My pet snake ate it!

And your cat?

it ate that too

Now they're the spookiest looking mosquito bites I've ever seen!!!

790 '**T**he Vampire's Victim' by E Drew Blood

791 '**W**itch in the Mirror' by Douglas Cracked

Ahhrrr BEAUTIFUL!

Every igloo starts with the first block of ice

792 '**I**gloo Building' by Art Tick

793 '**S**mashing Glass' by Eva Stone

801 **'S**ummer Bites' by Amos Quito

There's a very flat and very dead mosquito under there

802 **'V**egetable Gardening' by Rosa Cabbages

803 **'I**mprove Your Garden' by Anita Lawn

804 **'C**ontinental Breakfasts' by Roland Butter

805 **'P**ainting the Bathroom Brown' by Gus Troe

806 **'K**eep on Trying' by Percy Vere

807 **'C**heese and Salami Dishes' by Della Katessen

French Toast

814 '**S**easons Greetings' by Mary Christmas

815 '**R**eaching New Depths' by Beau Geepicker

816 '**T**he Ghost of a Witch' by Eve L Spirit

A GHOST OF A WITCH

817 '**H**ow to Feed Werewolves' by Nora Bone

818 '**T**errible Spells' by B Witcher

819 '**S**wallowing Dr Jekyll's Potion' by Iris Keverything

Sibling Rivalry

833 Did you hear about the time Eddie's sister tried to make a birthday cake?

The candles melted in the oven.

834 My sister went on a crash diet.

Is that why she looks like such a wreck?

835 Sister: *'Was our brother born on the highway?'*

Brother: *'No, why?'*

Sister: *'Because I heard that's where most accidents happen.'*

836 What do you call the cannibal who ate her father's sister?

An aunt-eater!

BURRPP! Oh excuse me!

Those relatives never did agree with me.

837 Teacher: *'How was your holiday, Penny?'*

Penny: *'Great. My brother and I spent the whole time on the beach, burying each other in the sand.'*

Teacher: *'That sounds like fun.'*

Penny: *'Daddy says we can go back next year and find him.'*

838 Why was the boy unhappy to win the prize for best costume at the Halloween party?

Because he just came to pick up his little sister!

839 Mother: *'Cathy, get your little sister's hat out of that puddle!'*

Cathy: *'I can't, Mum. She's got it strapped too tight under her chin.'*

840 James: *'My sister has lovely long hair, all down her back.'*
Will: *'Pity it's not on her head!'*

841 **W**hy doesn't your sister like peanuts?
Have you ever seen a skinny elephant?

842 Dad: *'Let's put your brother in the Science Fair, he'll do well.'*
Kid: *'Why?'*
Dad: *'Older siblings are like a parents' personal science fair - they're our experiments.'*

843 **M**y sister is so dim that she thinks a cartoon is something you sing in the car!

844 **D**octor, Doctor, my little brother thinks he's a computer.
Well bring him in so I can cure him.
I can't, I need to use him to finish my homework!

845 **W**hat makes you seasick?

Your little brother's vomit.

846 **C**harlie had a puppy on a leash. He met his brother Jim and said, *'I just got this puppy for our little brother.'*

'Really?' said Jim. *'That was good value as a swap!'*

847 **F**irst boy: *'My brother said he'd tell me everything he knows.'*

Second boy: *'He must have been speechless!'*

848 **D**id you hear about the girl who got her brother a birthday cake, but then couldn't figure out how to get the cake in the typewriter to write 'Happy Birthday'?

849 **D**an: *'My little brother is a real pain.'*

Nan: *'Things could be worse.'*

Dan: *'How?'*

Nan: *'He could be twins!'*

850 **F**irst boy: *'Does your brother keep himself clean?'*

Second boy: *'Oh, yes, he takes a bath every month, whether he needs one or not!'*

851 **B**ig brother: *'That planet over there is Mars.'*
Little brother: *'Then that other one must be Pa's.'*

852 **W**hy did your brother ask your father to sit in the freezer?

Because he wanted an ice-cold pop!

Doctor, Doctor . . .

853 Doctor, Doctor, my sister keeps thinking she's invisible.

Which sister?

854 Doctor, Doctor, I have a carrot growing out of my ear.

Amazing! How could that have happened?

I don't understand it – I planted cabbages in there!

855 Doctor, Doctor, I've spent so long at my computer that I now see double.

Well, walk around with one eye shut.

856 Doctor, Doctor, can I have a bottle of aspirin and a pot of glue?

Why?

Because I've got a splitting headache!

857 Doctor, Doctor, I think I've been bitten by a vampire.

Drink this glass of water.

Will it make me better?

No, but I'll be able to see if your neck leaks!

858 Doctor, Doctor, my son has swallowed my pen. What should I do?

Use a pencil until I get there.

859 **D**octor, Doctor, I think I'm a bell.

Take these, and if they don't help, give me a ring!

860 **D**octor, Doctor, I've got wind! Can you give me something?

Yes – here's a kite!

861 **D**octor, Doctor, I keep thinking I'm a dog.

Sit on the couch and we'll talk about it.

But I'm not allowed on the furniture!

862 **D**octor, Doctor, I think I'm a bridge.

What's come over you?

Oh, two cars, a large truck and a bus.

863 Doctor, Doctor, can I have a second opinion?

Of course, come back tomorrow.

864 Doctor, Doctor, when I press with my finger here . . . it hurts, and here . . . it hurts, and here . . . and here! What do you think is wrong with me?

Your finger's broken!

865 Doctor, Doctor, you have to help me out!

That's easily done, which way did you come in?

866 Doctor, Doctor, I keep thinking I'm God.

When did this start?

After I created the sun, then the earth . . .

867 **D**octor, Doctor, I feel like a spoon!

Well sit down and don't stir!

868 **D**octor, Doctor, I think I need glasses.

You certainly do – you've just walked into a restaurant!

869 **D**octor, Doctor, I've just swallowed a pen.

Well sit down and write your name!

870 **D**octor, Doctor, I feel like a dog.

Sit!

871 **D**octor, Doctor, I'm becoming invisible.

Yes, I can see you're not all there!

872 **D**octor, Doctor, will this ointment clear up my spots?

I never make rash promises!

873 **D**octor, Doctor,
everyone keeps
throwing me in
the garbage.

*Don't talk
rubbish!*

874 **D**octor, Doctor, I'm boiling up!

Just simmer down!

875 **D**octor, Doctor, I feel like a needle.

I see your point!

876 **D**octor, Doctor, how can I cure my sleepwalking?

Sprinkle tin-tacks on your bedroom floor!

A GUARANTEED CURE FOR SLEEPWALKING

877 **D**octor, Doctor,
I feel like a
racehorse.

*Take one of
these every four laps!*

878 **D**octor, Doctor, I
feel like a bee.

Buzz off, I'm busy!

879 **D**octor, Doctor, I
think I'm a burglar!

*Have you taken
anything for it?*

880 **D**octor, Doctor, I keep seeing an insect spinning.

Don't worry, it's just a bug that's going around.

881 **D**octor, Doctor, how can I stop my nose from
running?

Stick your foot out and trip it up!

882 **D**octor, Doctor, I'm having trouble with my breathing.

I'll give you something that will soon put a stop to that!

883 **D**octor, Doctor, I tend to flush a lot.

Don't worry, it's just a chain reaction.

884 **D**octor, Doctor, my baby looks just like his father.

Never mind – just as long as he's healthy.

885 **D**octor, Doctor, everyone thinks I'm a liar.

Well, that's hard to believe!

886 **D**octor, Doctor, what did the X-ray of my head show?

Absolutely nothing!

887 **D**octor, Doctor, I keep thinking I'm a mosquito.
Go away, sucker!

888 **D**octor, Doctor, I think I'm a moth.
So why did you come around then?
Well, I saw this light at the window . . .

889 **D**octor, Doctor, I keep thinking I'm a spider.
What a web of lies!

890 **D**octor, Doctor, I keep painting myself gold.
Don't worry, it's just a gilt complex.

891 **D**octor, Doctor, I think I'm a rubber band.

Why don't you stretch yourself out on the couch there, and tell me all about it?

892 **D**octor, Doctor, everyone keeps ignoring me.

Next please!

893 **D**octor, Doctor, I keep thinking I'm a computer.

My goodness, you'd better come to my surgery right away!

I can't, my power cable won't reach that far!

894 **D**octor, Doctor, I feel like a pair of curtains.

Oh, pull yourself together!

895 **D**octor, Doctor, I think I'm a computer.

How long have you felt like this?

Ever since I was switched on!

896 **D**octor, Doctor, I don't think I'm a computer any more. Now I think I'm a desk.

You're just letting things get on top of you.

897 **D**octor, Doctor, I keep thinking there's two of me.

One at a time please!

898 **D**octor, Doctor, some days I feel like a teepee and other days I feel like a wigwam.

You're too tents!

899 **D**octor, Doctor, my little boy has just swallowed a roll of film.

Hmmm. Let's hope nothing develops!

900 Doctor, Doctor, I can't get to sleep.

Sit on the edge of the bed and you'll soon drop off.

901 Doctor, Doctor, I feel like a pack of cards.

I'll deal with you later!

902 Doctor, Doctor, I snore so loud that I keep myself awake.

Sleep in another room, then.

903 Doctor, Doctor, I've a split personality.

Well, you'd better both sit down, then.

904 Doctor, Doctor, I think I'm a yo-yo.

You're stringing me along!

905 **D**octor, Doctor, I keep thinking I'm a vampire.

Necks, please!

906 **D**octor, Doctor, I swallowed a bone.

Are you choking?

No, I really did!

Whatever it was... you ate it whole! Was it some kind of DINOSAUR?

907 **D**octor, Doctor, I dream there are zombies under my bed. What can I do?

Saw the legs off your bed.

908 **D**octor, Doctor, I think I'm a woodworm.

How boring for you!

909 **D**octor, Doctor, I think I'm an electric eel.

That's shocking!

910 Doctor, Doctor, I think I'm a nit.

Will you get out of my hair?

911 Doctor, Doctor, I've broken my arm in two places.

Well don't go back there again.

912 Doctor, Doctor, I think I'm a butterfly.

Will you say what you mean and stop flitting about!

913 Doctor, Doctor, I think I'm a frog.

What's wrong with that?

I think I'm going to croak!

914 Doctor, Doctor, I think I'm a snake, about to shed its skin.

Why don't you go behind the screen and slip into something more comfortable, then!

915 Doctor, Doctor, these pills you gave me for BO . . .

What's wrong with them?

They keep slipping out from under my arms!

916 Doctor, Doctor, my husband smells like a fish.

Poor sole!

917 Doctor, Doctor, my sister thinks she's a lift.

Well tell her to come in.

I can't, she doesn't stop at this floor!

918 Doctor, Doctor, I think I'm a caterpillar.

Don't worry, you'll soon change.

With Friends Like These

919 **G**irl to friend: *'I'm sorry, I won't be able to come out tonight. I promised Dad I'd stay in and help him with my homework . . .'*

920 **W**hy are giraffes good friends to have?

Because they stick their necks out for you.

921 **W**hich of the witches' friends eats the fastest?

The goblin.

922 **K**nock knock.

Who's there?

Doris.

Doris who?

The Doris locked so let me in.

923 **K**nock knock.

Who's there?

Jilly!

Jilly who?

Jilly out here, so let me in!

924 **K**nock knock.

Who's there?

Gable!

Gable who?

Gable to leap tall buildings in a single bound!

925 **K**nock knock.

Who's there?

Abe!

Abe who?

Abe C D E F G H . . .

926 **H**ow does a skeleton call his friends?

On a telebone.

927 **K**nock knock.
Who's there?
James!
James who?
James people play!

928 **K**nock knock.
Who's there?
Effie.
Effie who?
Effie'd known you were coming he'd have stayed at home.

929 **K**nock knock.
Who's there?
Eliza.
Eliza who?
Eliza wake at night thinking about you.

930   **K**nock knock.

Who's there?

Evan.

Evan who?

Evan you should know who I am.

931   **J**ane was telling her friend about her vacation in Switzerland. Her friend asked, *'What did you think of the beautiful scenery?'*

'Oh, I couldn't see much,' said Jane. *'There were too many mountains in the way.'*

932   **K**nock knock.

Who's there?

Hugo.

Hugo who?

Hugo one way, I'll go the other.

933 **M**r Cannibal: 'I've brought a friend home for dinner.'

Mrs Cannibal: *'But I've already made a stew.'*

934 **'W**hat shall we play today?' Tanya asked her best friend, Emma.

'Let's play schools,' said Emma.

'Okay,' said Tanya. 'But I'm going to be absent.'

935 **H**ow many teenage girls does it take to change a light bulb?

One, but she'll be on the phone for five hours telling all her friends about it.

936 **W**hy do demons and ghouls get on so well?
Because demons are a ghoul's best friend.

937 **K**nock knock.
Who's there?
Celeste.
Celeste who?
Celeste time I come round here.

938 **K**nock knock.
Who's there?
Rose.
Rose who?
Rose early to come and see you.

939 **K**nock knock.
Who's there?
Roxanne.
Roxanne who?
Roxanne pebbles are all over your garden.

940 **K**nock knock.
Who's there?
Colin.
Colin who?
Colin all cars. Colin all cars.

941 **W**hen is the cheapest time to phone friends?
When they're not home.

942 **K**nock knock.
Who's there?
Jim!
Jim who?
Jim mind if we
all come in!

943 **K**nock knock.
Who's there?
Jimmy!
Jimmy who?
Jimmy a little kiss on the cheek!

944 **K**nock knock.
Who's there?
Gary!
Gary who?
Gary on smiling!

Just a
happy guy

945 **K**nock knock.
Who's there?
Adam!
Adam who?
Adam up and tell me the total!

946 **K**nock knock.
Who's there?
Alan!
Alan who?
Alan a good cause!

947 **K**nock knock.
Who's there?
Jo!
Jo who?
Jo jump in the lake!

948 **K**nock knock.
Who's there?
Carlotta!
Carlotta who?
Carlotta trouble when it breaks down!

Spooky

949 **W**here do ghosts go to learn to frighten people?
Swooniversity.

950 **W**hy did the ghost pick its nose?
It was full of boo-gers.

951 **H**ow does a witch make scrambled eggs?
She holds the pan and gets two friends to make the stove shake with fright.

What's say I just turn you into a cute cuddly little toad

952 **W**hy did the zombie call in sick?
He was feeling rotten.

953 **W**hat's a witch's favourite movie?
Broom with a View.

954 **W**hat do you call a motorbike belonging to a witch?

A broooooooooom stick!

955 **W**hat vehicles race at the Witch Formula One Grand Prix?

Vroomsticks.

956 **W**ho did the witch call when her broom was stolen?

The flying squad.

957 **W**hat story do little witches like to hear at bedtime?

Ghoul deluxe and the three scares!

958 **W**hat happened when the gravediggers went on strike?

Their job was done by a skeleton crew.

959　How does a witch tell the time?

With a witch watch!

960　Why did the witch put her broom in the washing machine?

She wanted a clean sweep!

961　What noise does a witch's breakfast cereal make?

Snap, cackle and pop!

962　Did you hear about the boy who saw a witch riding on a broomstick?

He asked, 'What are you doing on that?'

She replied, 'My sister's got the vacuum cleaner!'

963　Why couldn't the witch race her horse in the Witch Derby?

Because it was having a spell.

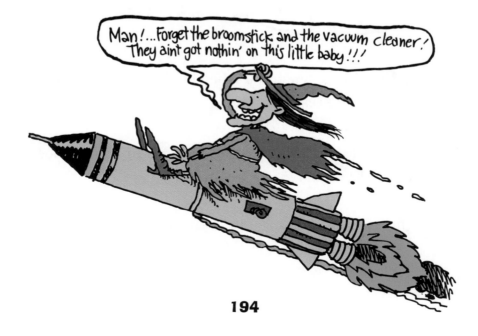

964 **F**irst witch: *'My, hasn't your little girl grown!'*

Second witch: *'Yes, she's certainly gruesome.'*

965 **H**ow does a witchdoctor ask a girl to dance?

'Voodoo like to dance with me?'

966 **W**hy did the witches go on strike?

Because they wanted sweeping reforms.

967 **W**hy do witches get good bargains?

Because they're good at haggling.

968 **W**hat do you get when you cross a heater with a witch?

A hot spell.

969 **W**hat do you get when you cross a witch and a skunk?

An ugly smell.

970 **H**ow do you make a witch itch?

Take away the 'w'.

971 **W**hat do you do if you're surrounded by a witch, a werewolf, a vampire and two ghosts?

Hope you're at a fancy dress party.

972 **W**hat do ghosts do to keep fit?

They hire an exercisist.

973 **W**here do monsters send their clothes for cleaning?

The dry screamers.

974 **W**ho is a ghost's favourite singer?

Mighoul Jackson.

975 **W**here do ghosts go swimming?

In the Dead Sea.

976 **W**hat kind of plate does a skeleton eat off?

Bone china.

977 **H**ow do you know a monster is in love when it farts?

Because its butt is blowing kisses.

978 **I**f you cross a witch's cat with Father Christmas, what do you get?

Santa Claws.

979 **W**hat trees do ghosts like best?

Ceme-trees.

980 **W**here do Australian ghosts live?

In the Northern Terror-tory.

981 **W**hich ghost ate the three bears' porridge?

Ghouldilocks.

982 **W**here do cannibals work?

At head office.

983 **W**hich ghost is President of France?

Charles de Ghoul.

984 **W**ho is big and hairy, wears a dress and climbs the Empire State Building?

Queen Kong.

985 **W**hy did the ghost go to jail?

For driving without due scare and attention.

986 **W**hat do ghosts do in the January sales?

Go bargain haunting.

987   **D**id you hear about the little spook who couldn't sleep at night because his brother kept telling him human stories?

988   **W**hy are ghosts always tired?

Because they are dead on their feet.

989   **W**ho won the running race between Count Dracula and Countess Dracula?

It was neck and neck.

990   **W**hat should you say when you meet a ghost?

How do you boo, Sir, how do you boo?

991 **W**hat did the mother ghost say to the baby ghost?

Put your boos and shocks on!

992 **W**hen do ghosts usually appear?

Just before someone screams!

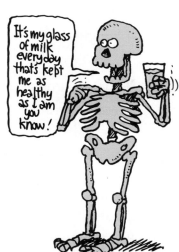

993 **W**hy do skeletons drink milk?

Because it's good for the bones.

994 **D**id you hear about the ghouls' favourite hotel?

It had running rot and mould!

995 **W**ho speaks at the ghosts' press conference?

The spooksperson!

996 **W**hat is Count Dracula's favourite snack?

A fangfurter!

997 **W**hat do ghosts eat for breakfast?

Dreaded wheat!

998 **W**hat is a ghost's favourite dessert?

Boo-Berry pie with I-scream!

999 **W**hy are graveyards so noisy?

Because of all the coffin!

1000 **W**hat do you get if you cross a ghost with a packet of chips?

Snacks that go crunch in the night!

1001 **W**hat do Native American ghosts sleep in?

A creepy teepee!